First Position Scale Studies

for the Viola book one

by Cassia Harvey

Contents

C Major: First Octave	2
G Major: First Octave	6
D Major: Second Octave	10
F Major: First Octave	14
C Major: Second Octave	18
E-Flat Major: First Octave	22
B-Flat Major: First Octave	26
D Major: First Octave	30
A Major: First Octave	34
Scales to Play With Vibrato	38
Fast Scale Studies	42
Major Scales in First Position	48
Major Arpeggios in First Position	51

CHP318

©2017 by C. Harvey Publications All Rights Reserved.

www.charveypublications.com - print books
www.learnstrings.com - PDF downloadable books
www.harveystringarrangements.com - chamber music

C Major: First Octave

Cassia Harvey

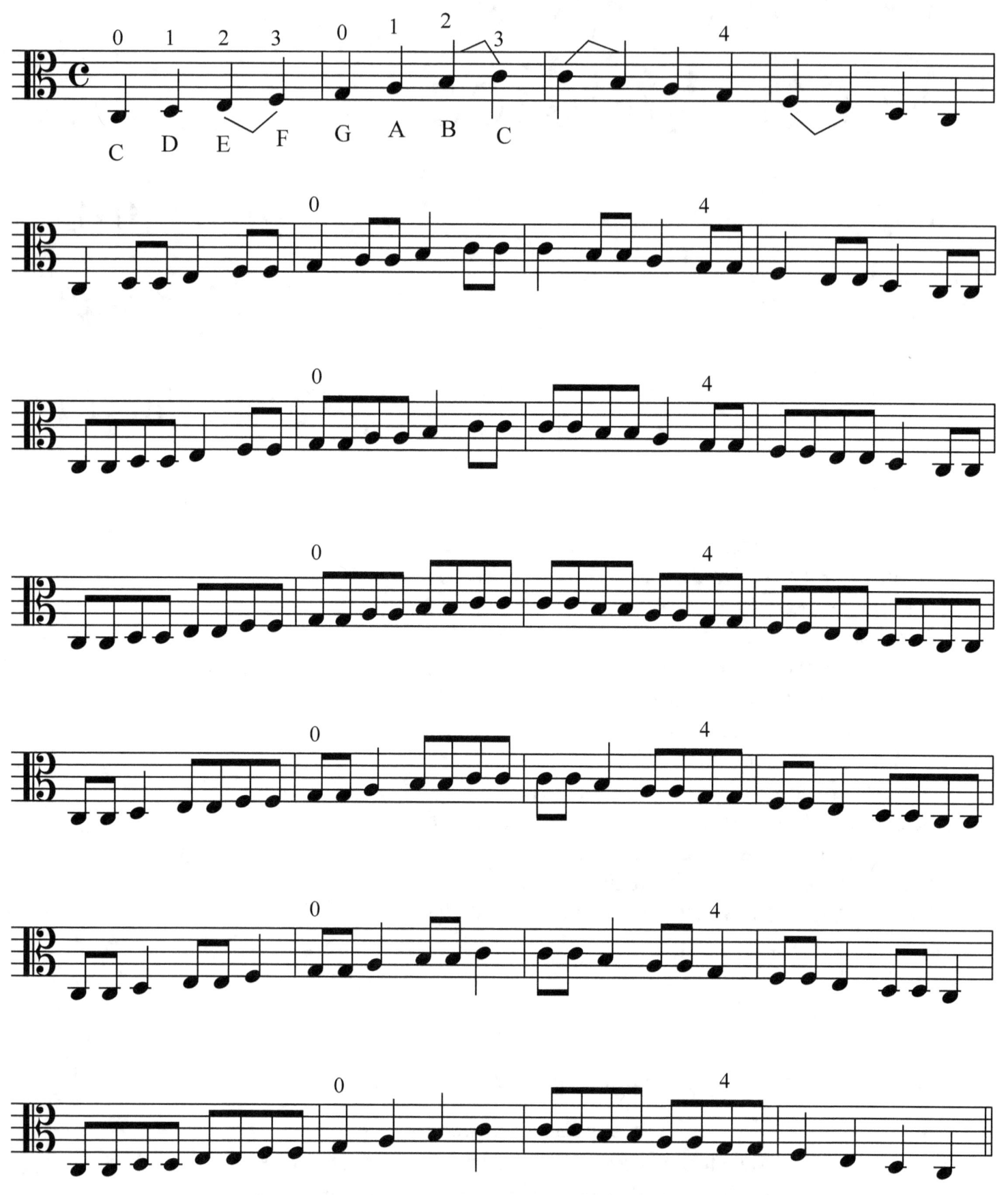

©2017 C. Harvey Publications All Rights Reserved.

First Position Scale Studies for the Viola, Book One

Slurs

©2017 C. Harvey Publications All Rights Reserved.

Scale Rhythms

Dotted Quarter Note Rhythms

G Major: First Octave

©2017 C. Harvey Publications All Rights Reserved.

First Position Scale Studies for the Viola, Book One

Slurs

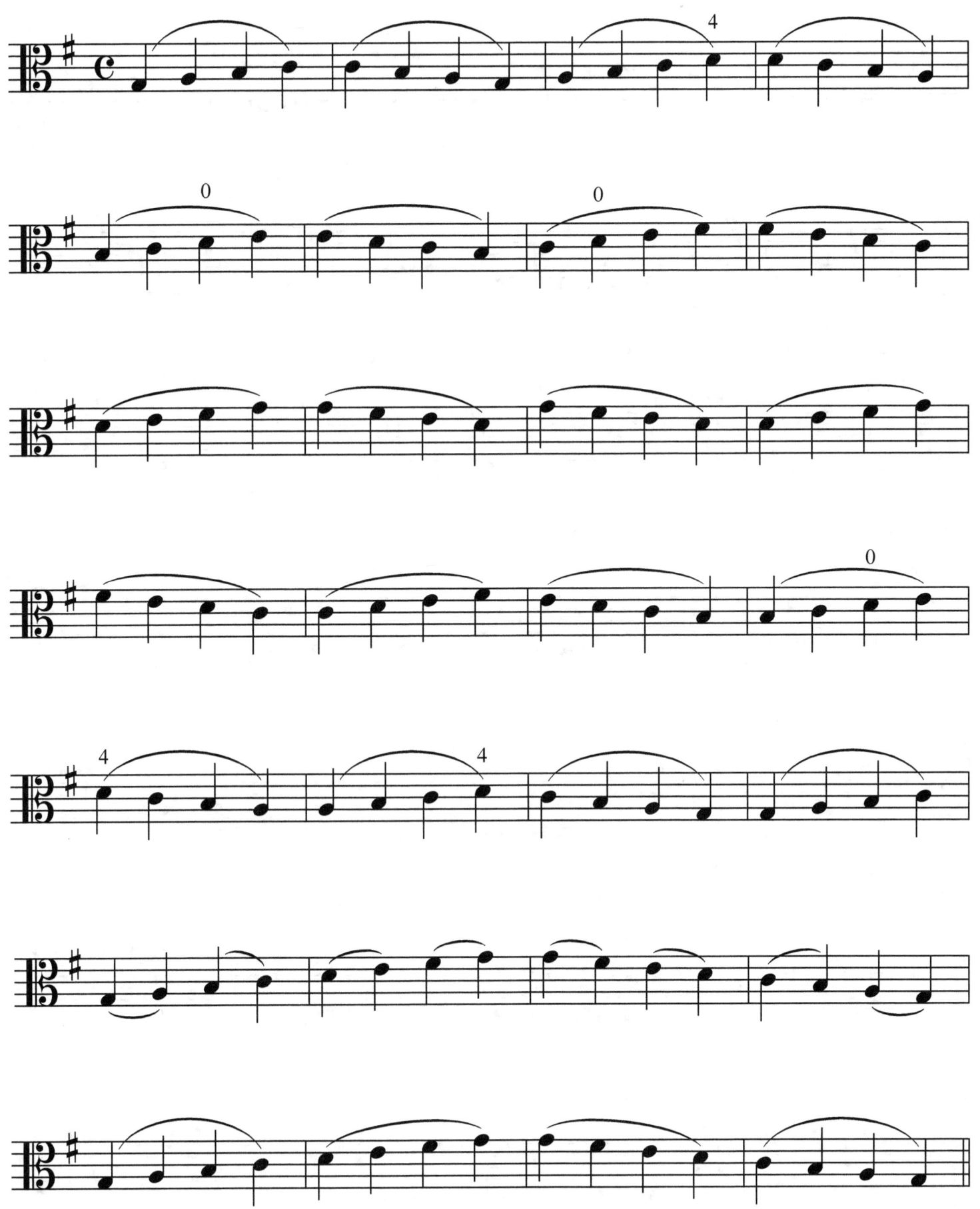

Scale Rhythms

6/8 Timing

D Major: Second Octave

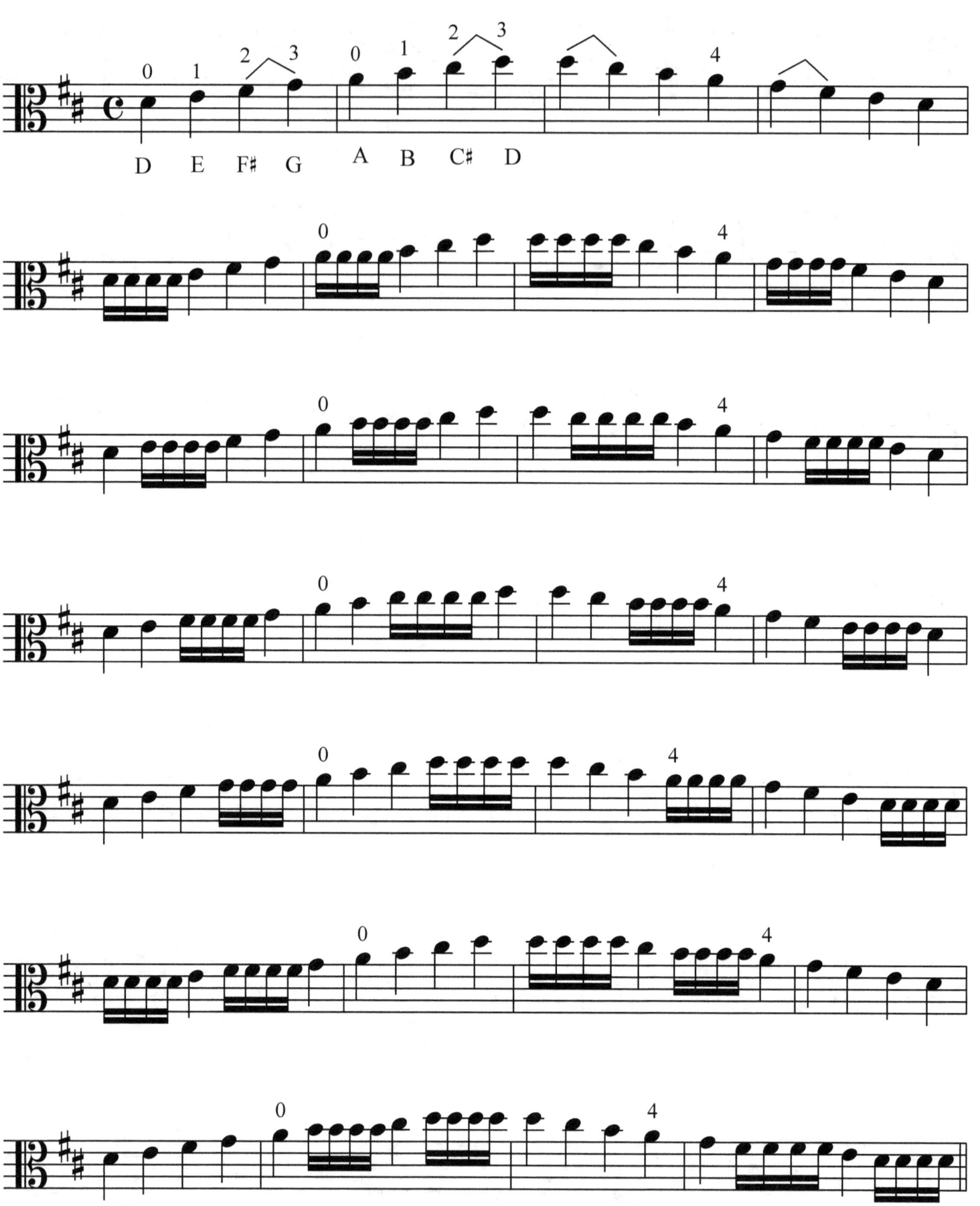

Slurs in 3/4

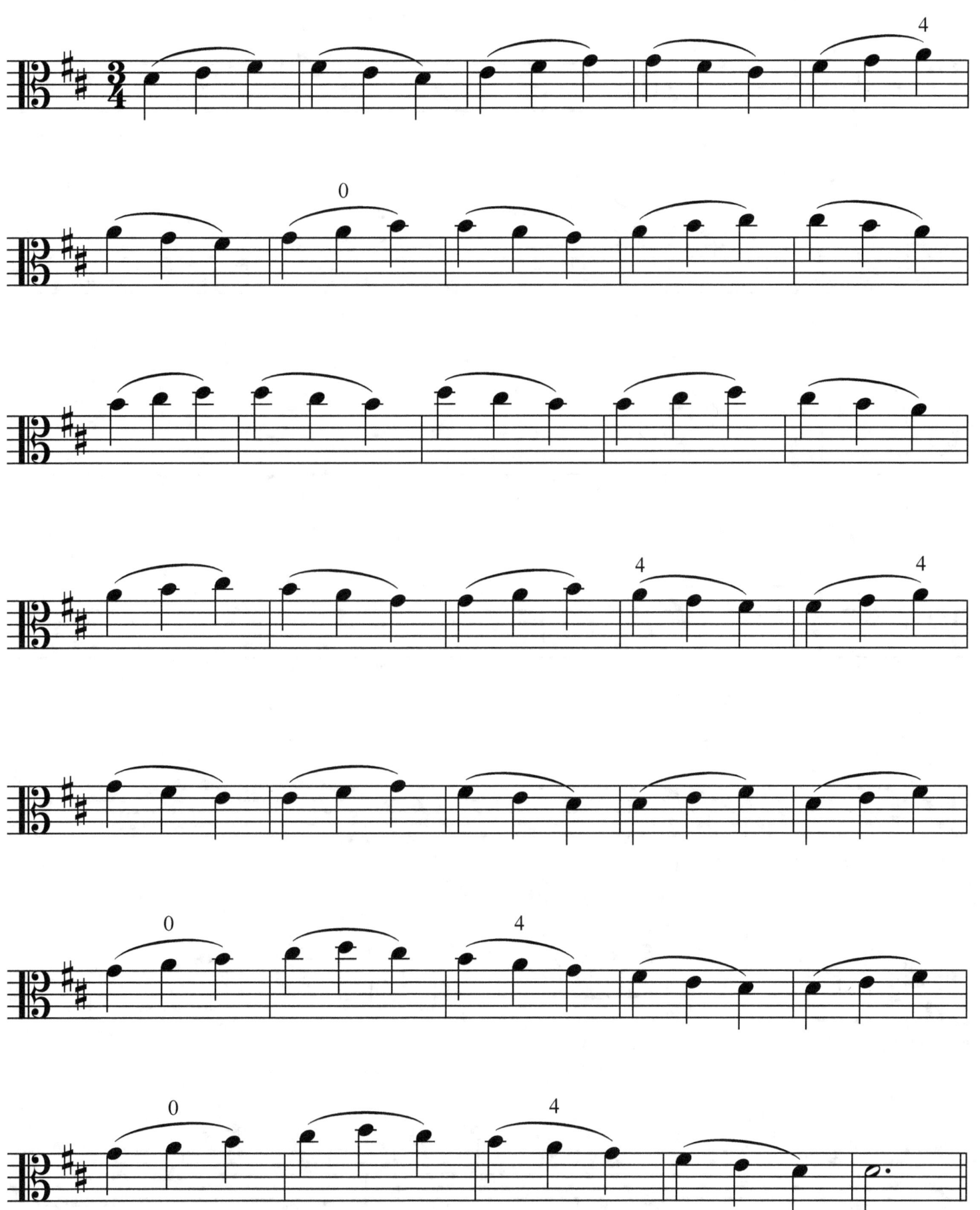

Scale Rhythms

First Position Scale Studies for the Viola, Book One

Trills

F Major: First Octave

Slurs

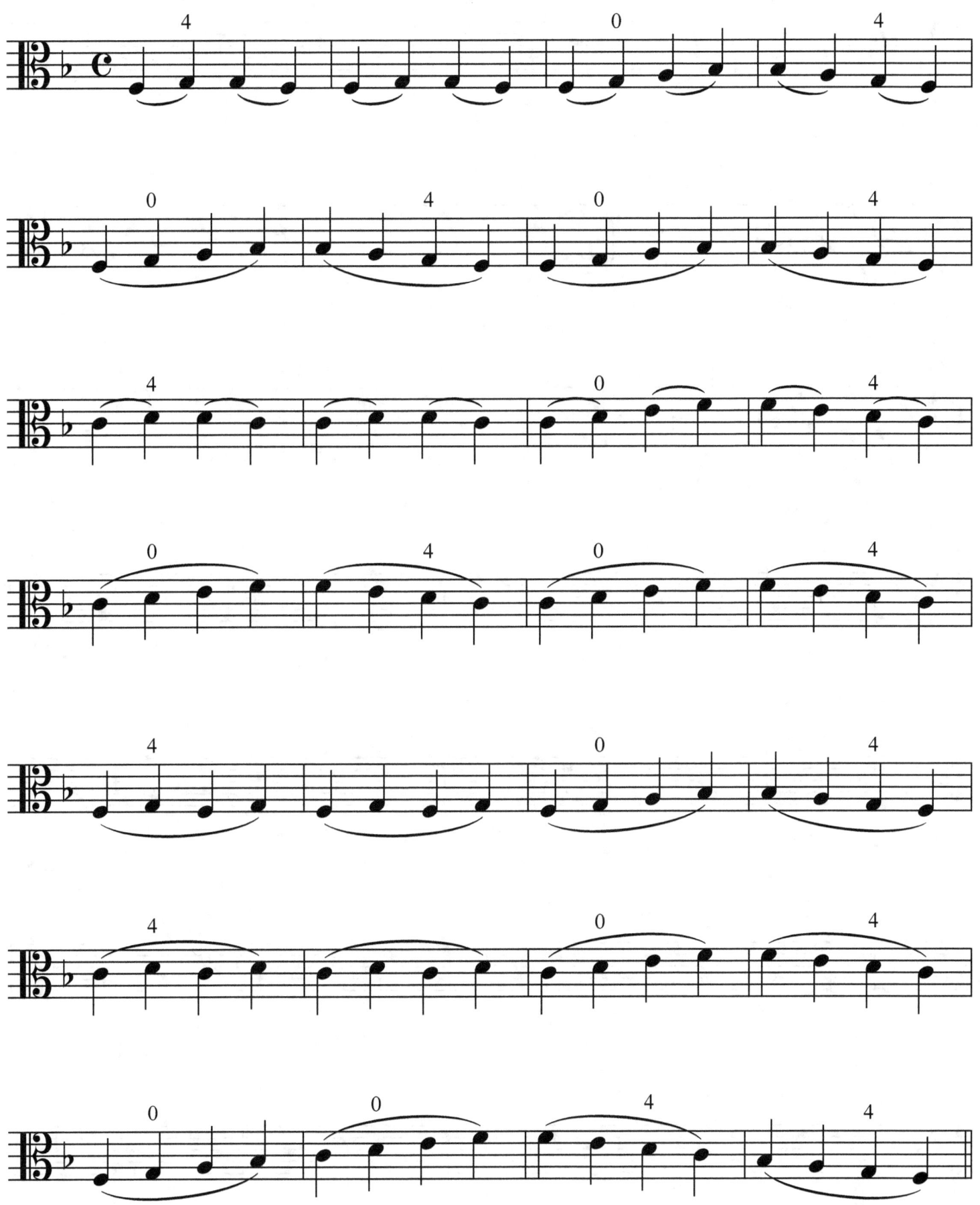

Dotted Quarter Note Rhythms

First Position Scale Studies for the Viola, Book One

6/8 Timing

©2017 C. Harvey Publications All Rights Reserved.

C Major: Second Octave

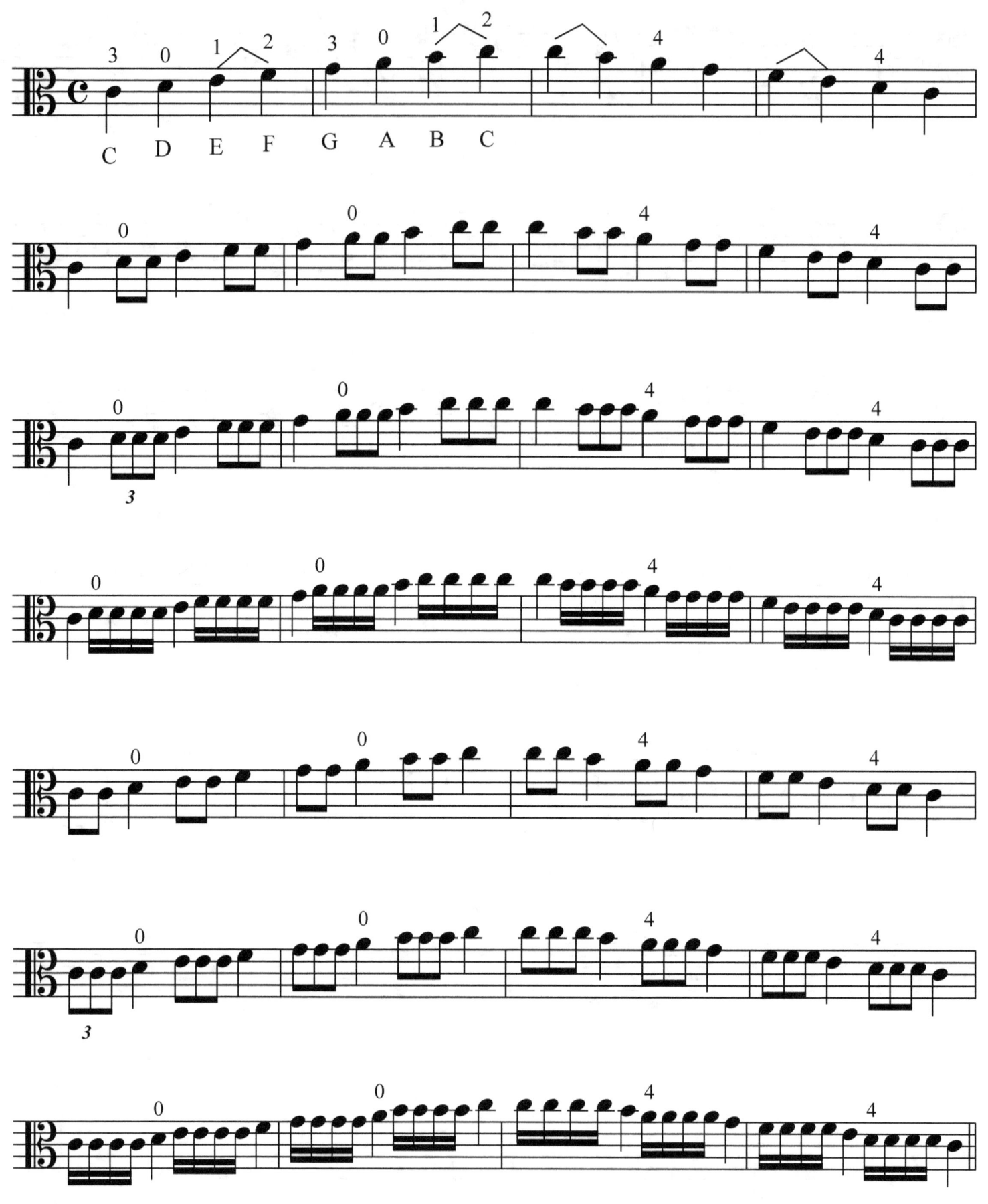

Slurs

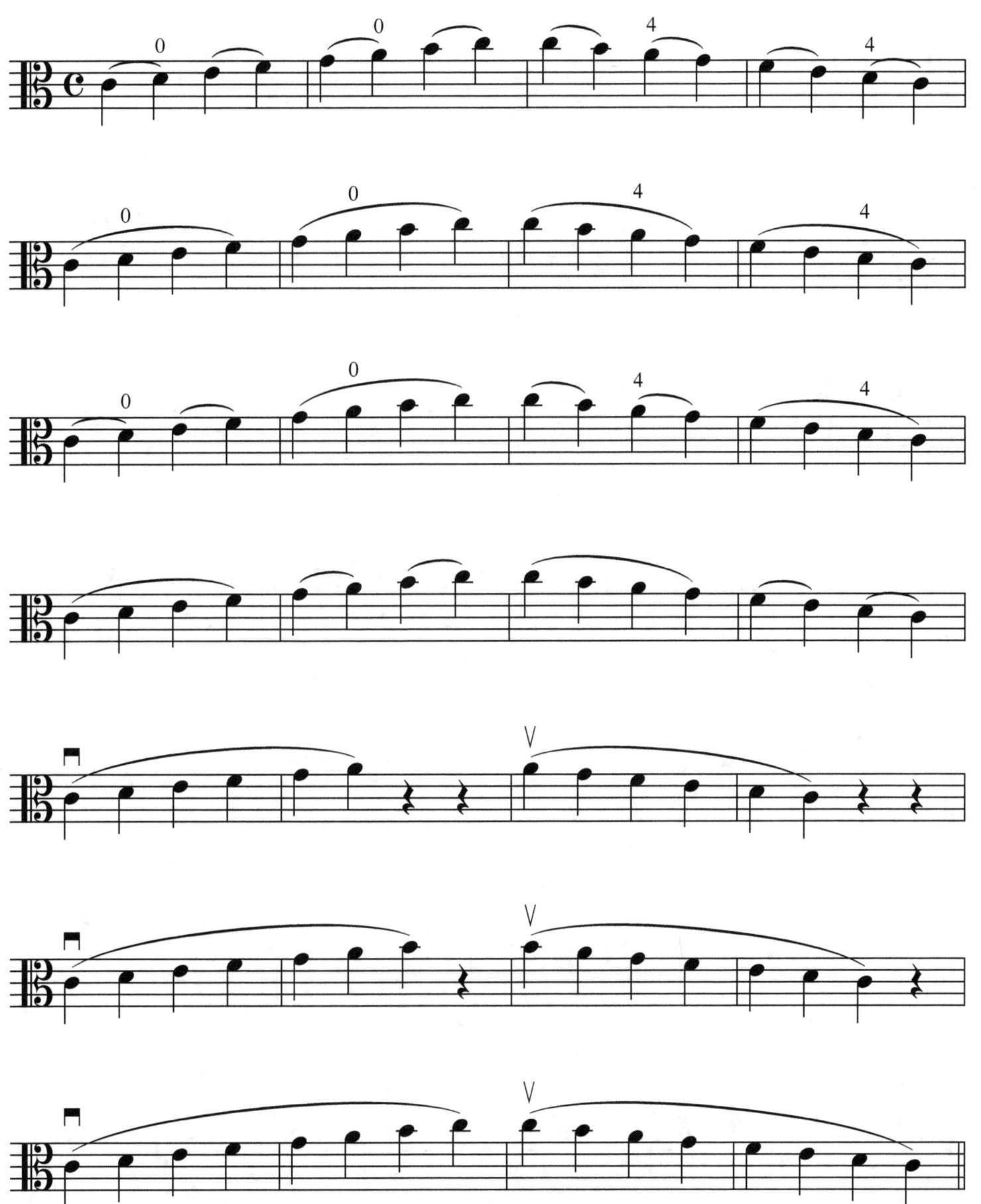

Dotted Quarter Note Rhythms

First Position Scale Studies for the Viola, Book One

6/8 Timing

E♭ Major: First Octave

First Position Scale Studies for the Viola, Book One

Scale Rhythms

©2017 C. Harvey Publications All Rights Reserved.

Slurs

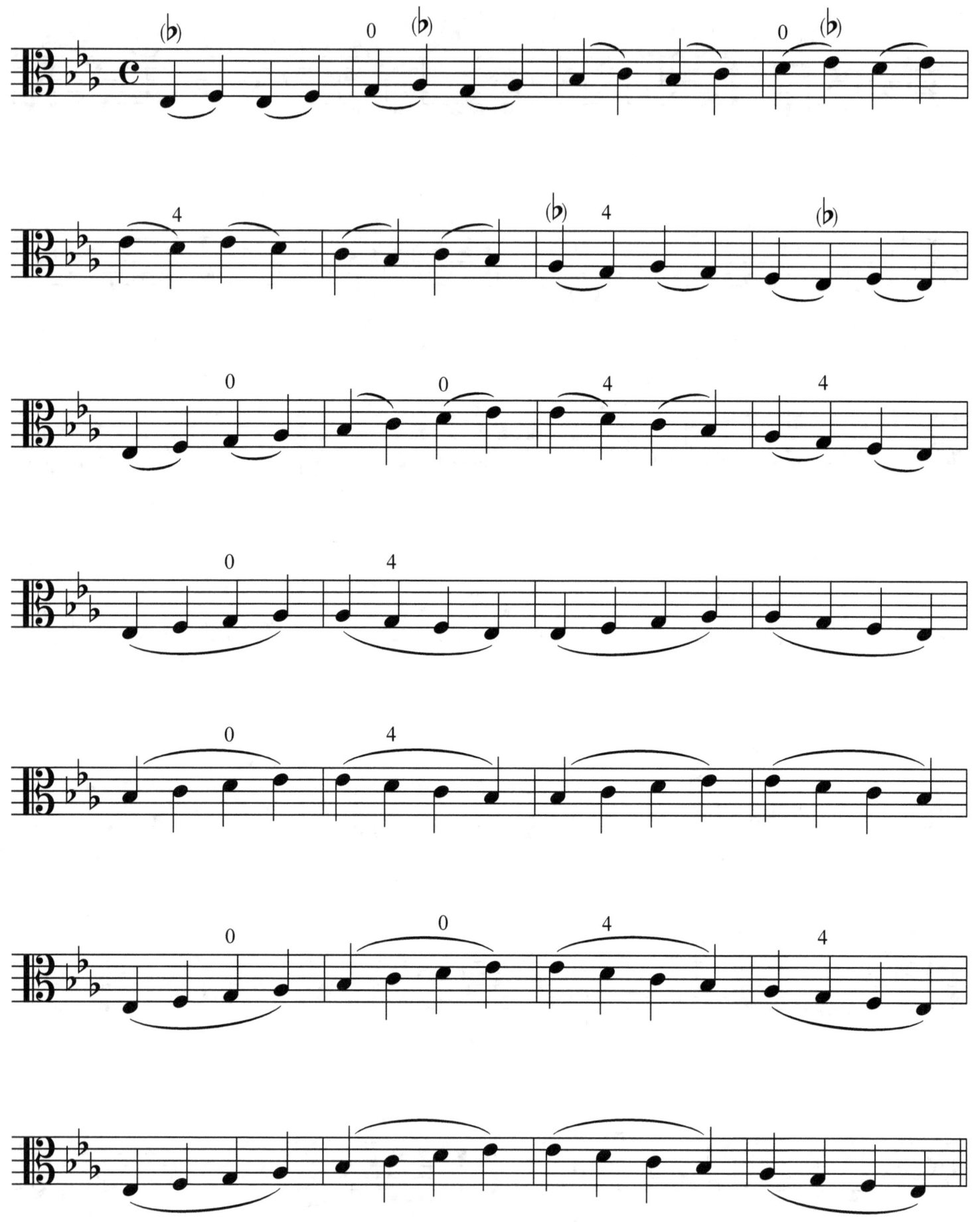

First Position Scale Studies for the Viola, Book One

Scale Finger Workout

B♭ Major: First Octave

Slurs

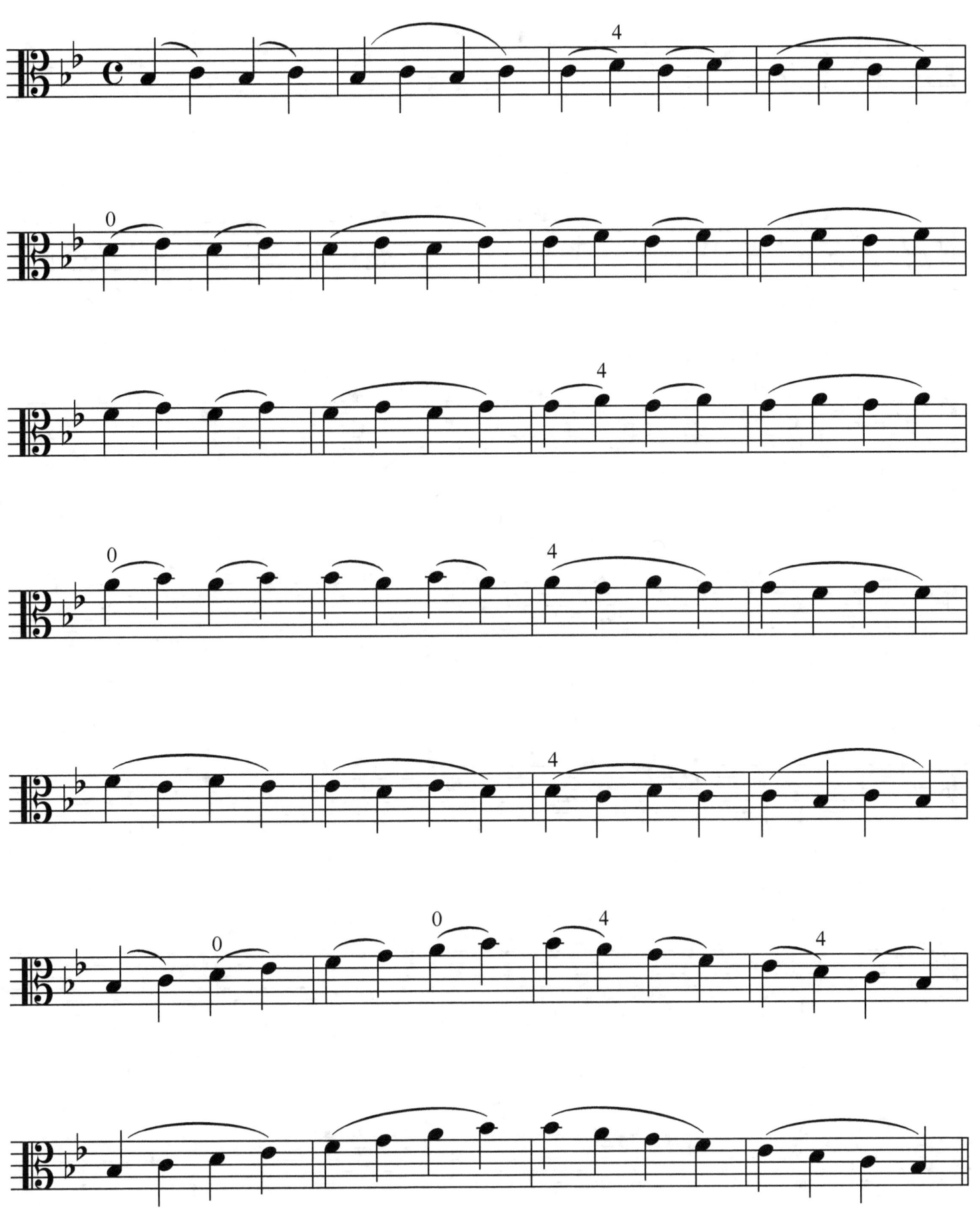

Dotted Quarter Note Rhythms

3/4 Timing

D Major: First Octave

Slurs

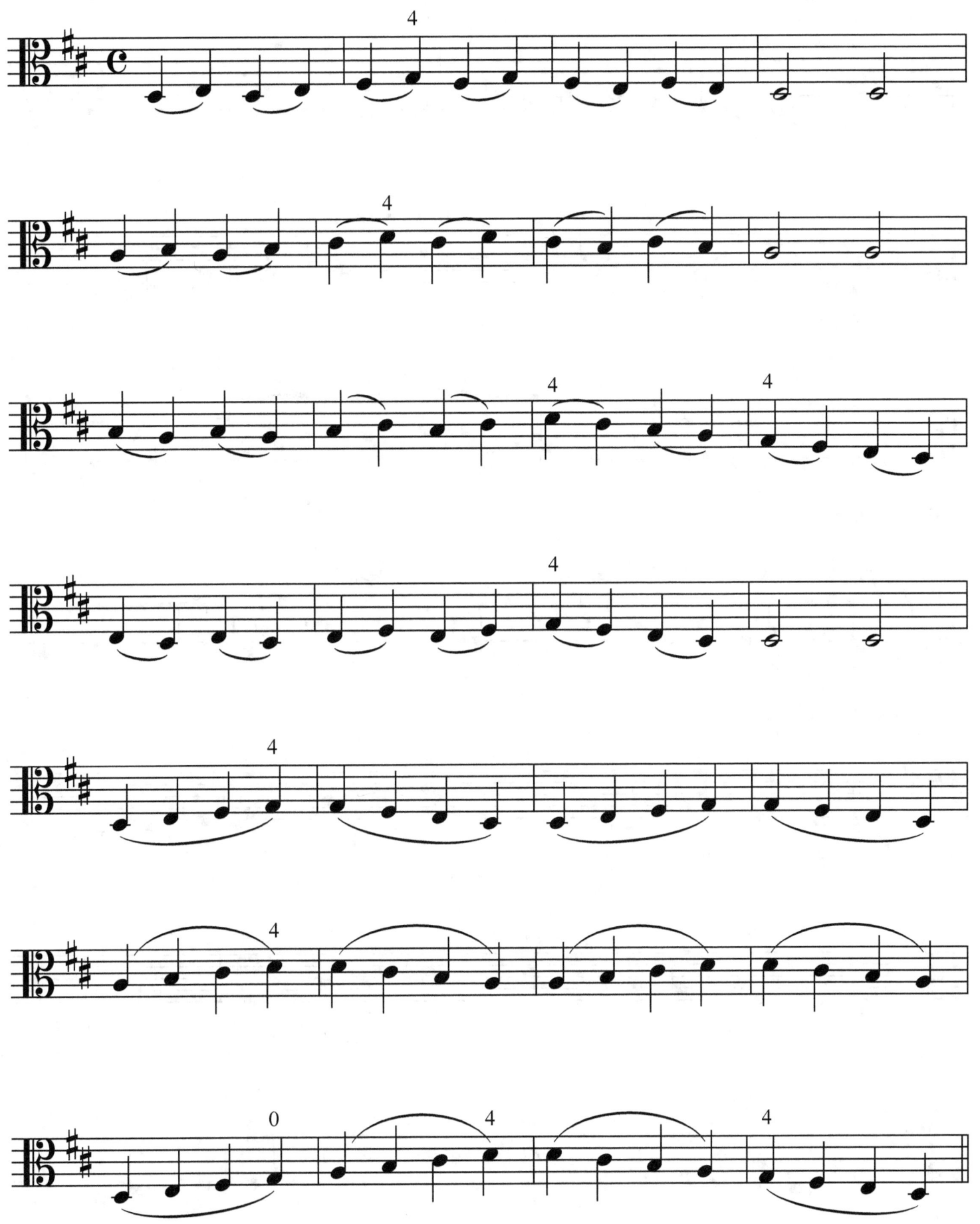

Scale Rhythms

Slurs in 3/4 Timing

A Major: First Octave

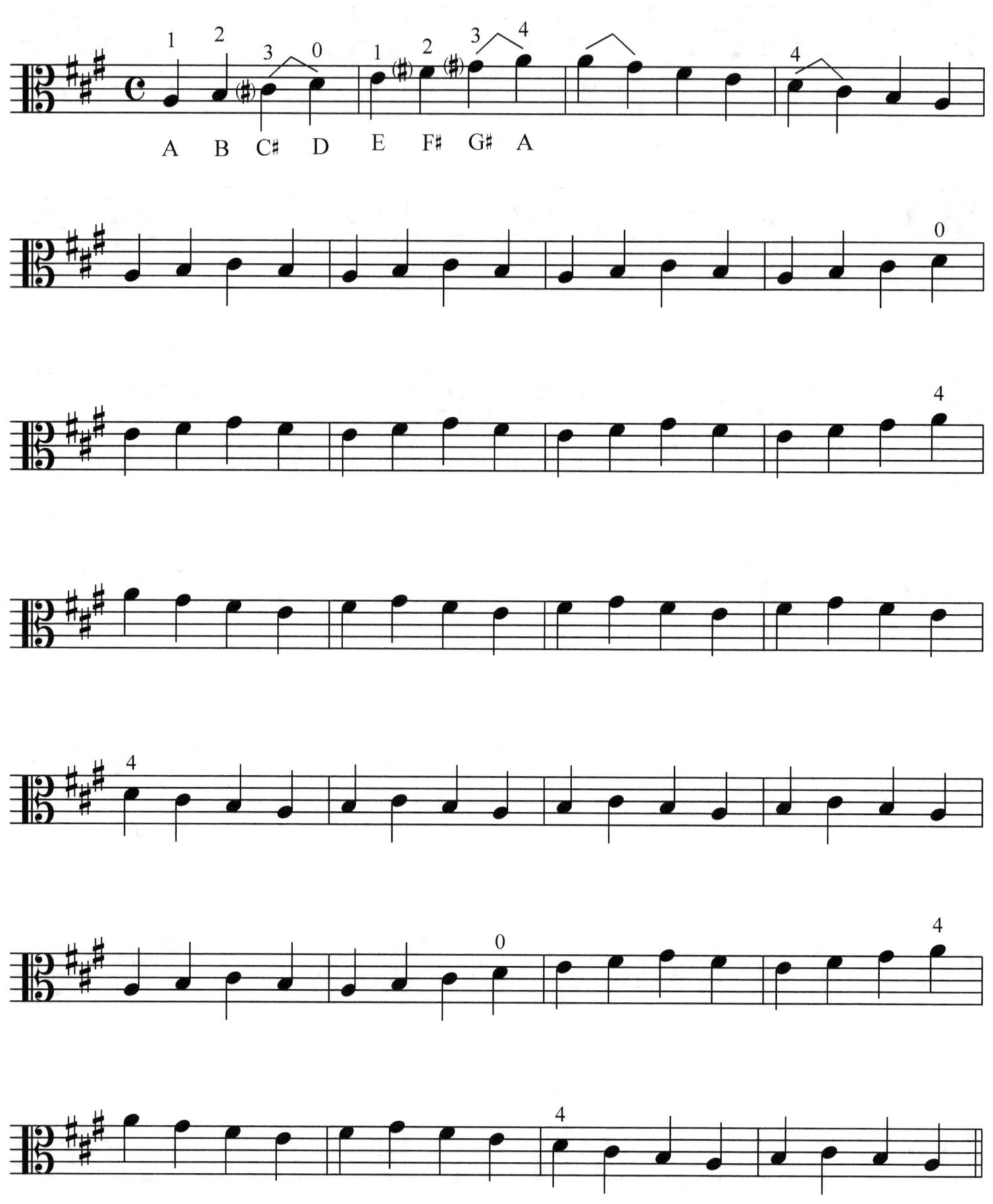

First Position Scale Studies for the Viola, Book One

Slurs

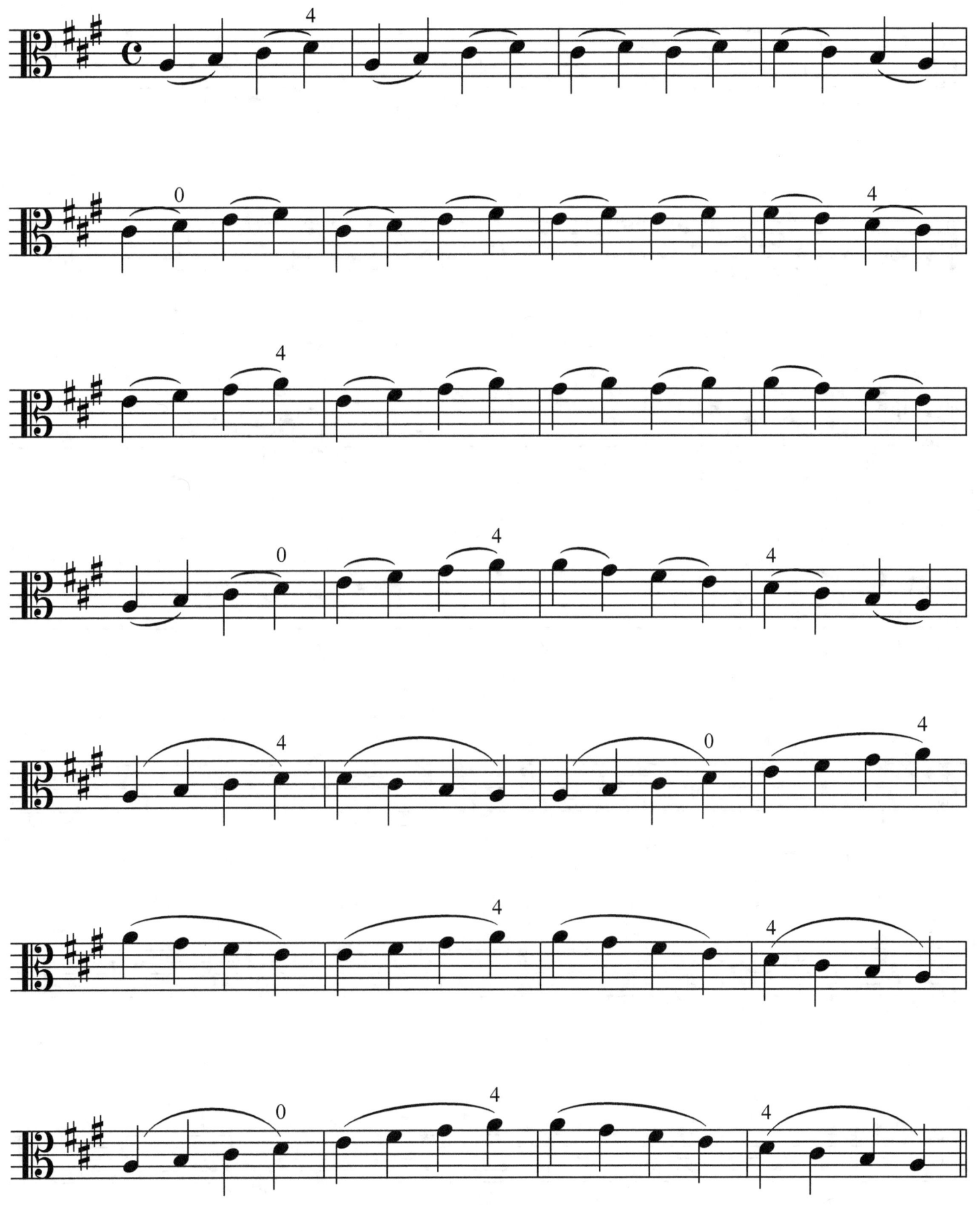

Scale Rhythms

First Position Scale Studies for the Viola, Book One

6/8 Timing

Scales to play with Vibrato

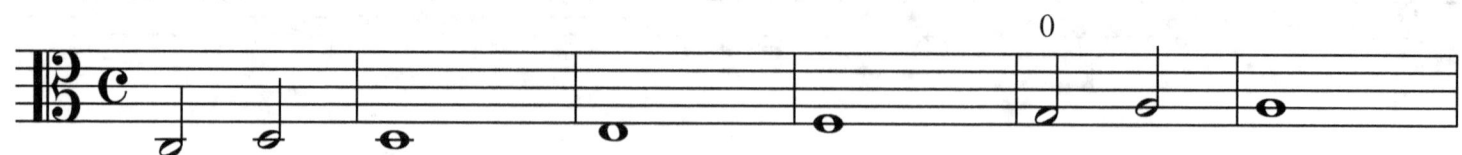
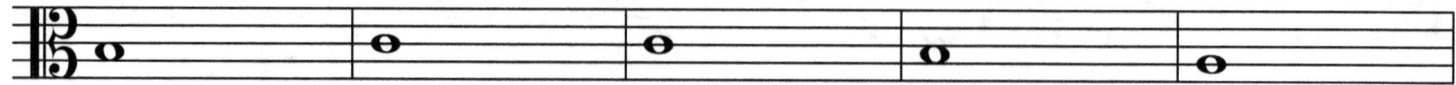
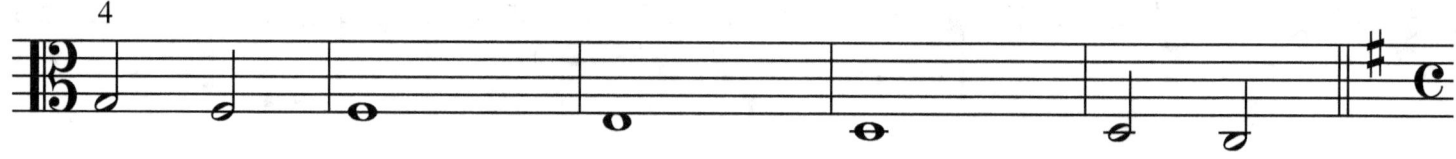

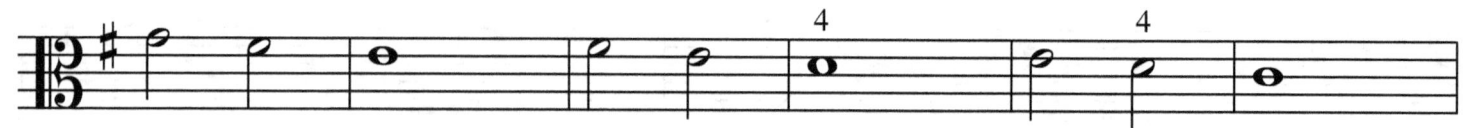

©2017 C. Harvey Publications All Rights Reserved.

First Position Scale Studies for the Viola, Book One

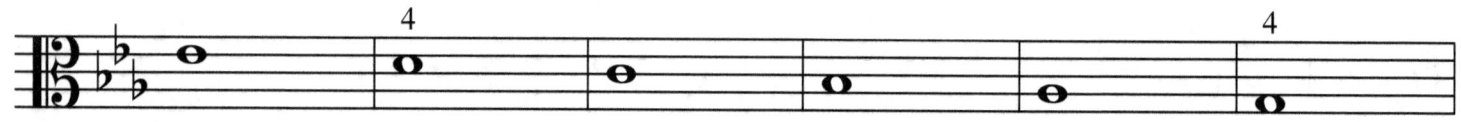

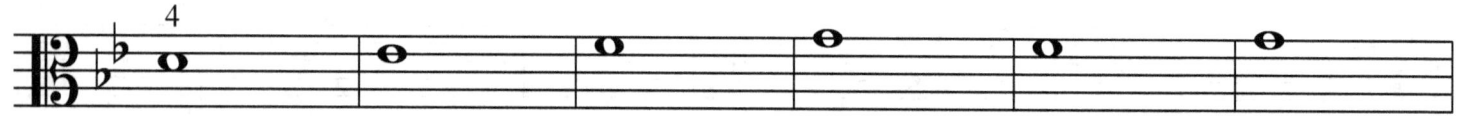
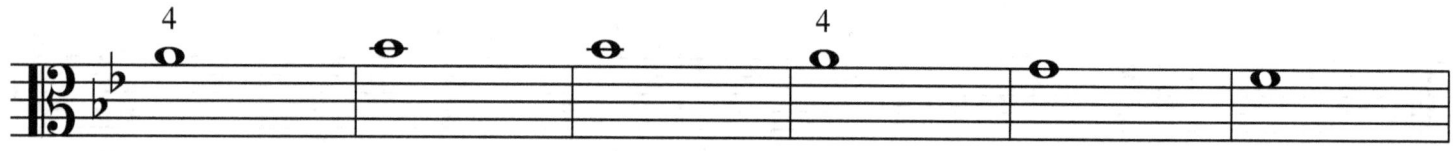

First Position Scale Studies for the Viola, Book One 41

Fast Scale Studies

First Position Scale Studies for the Viola, Book One

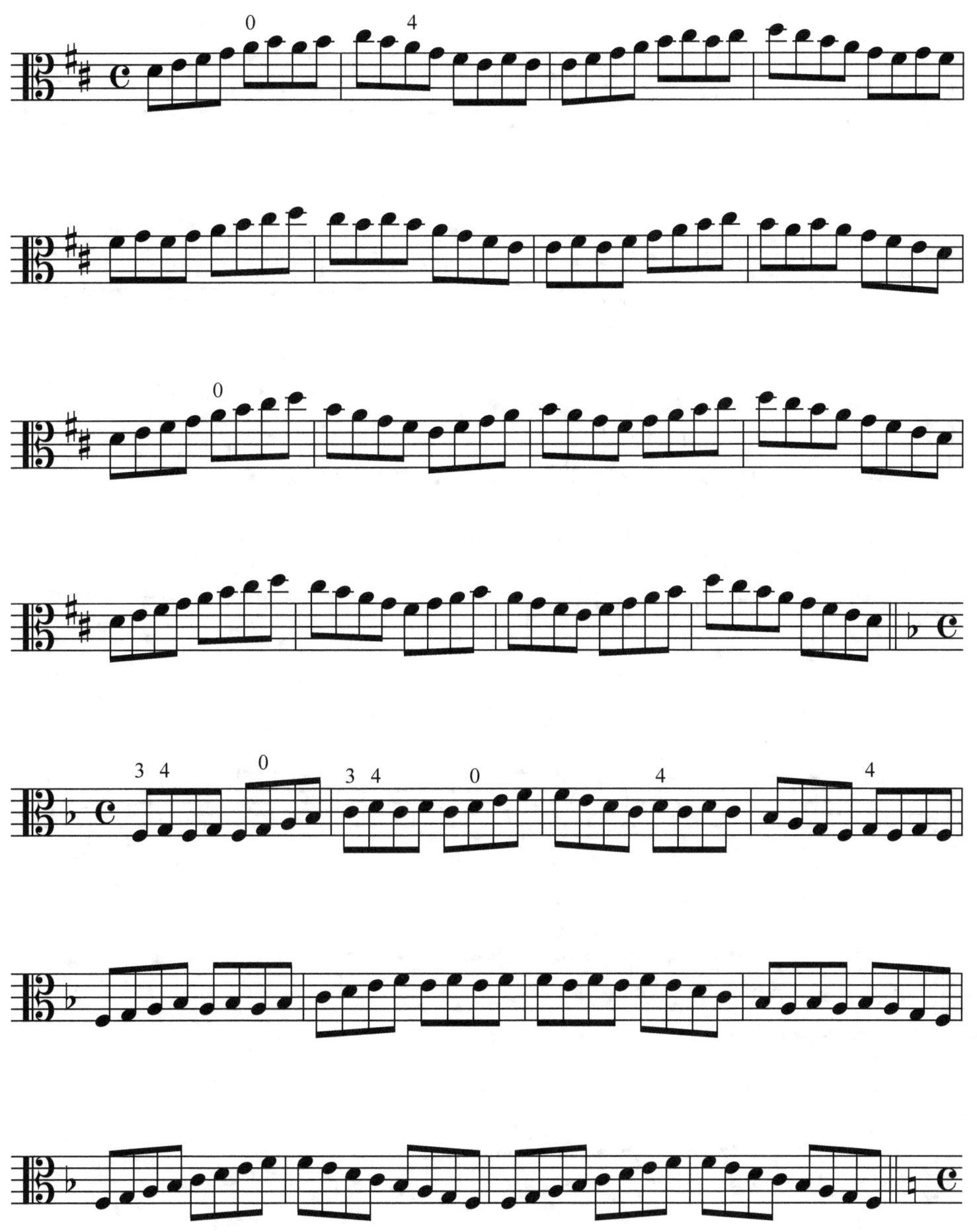

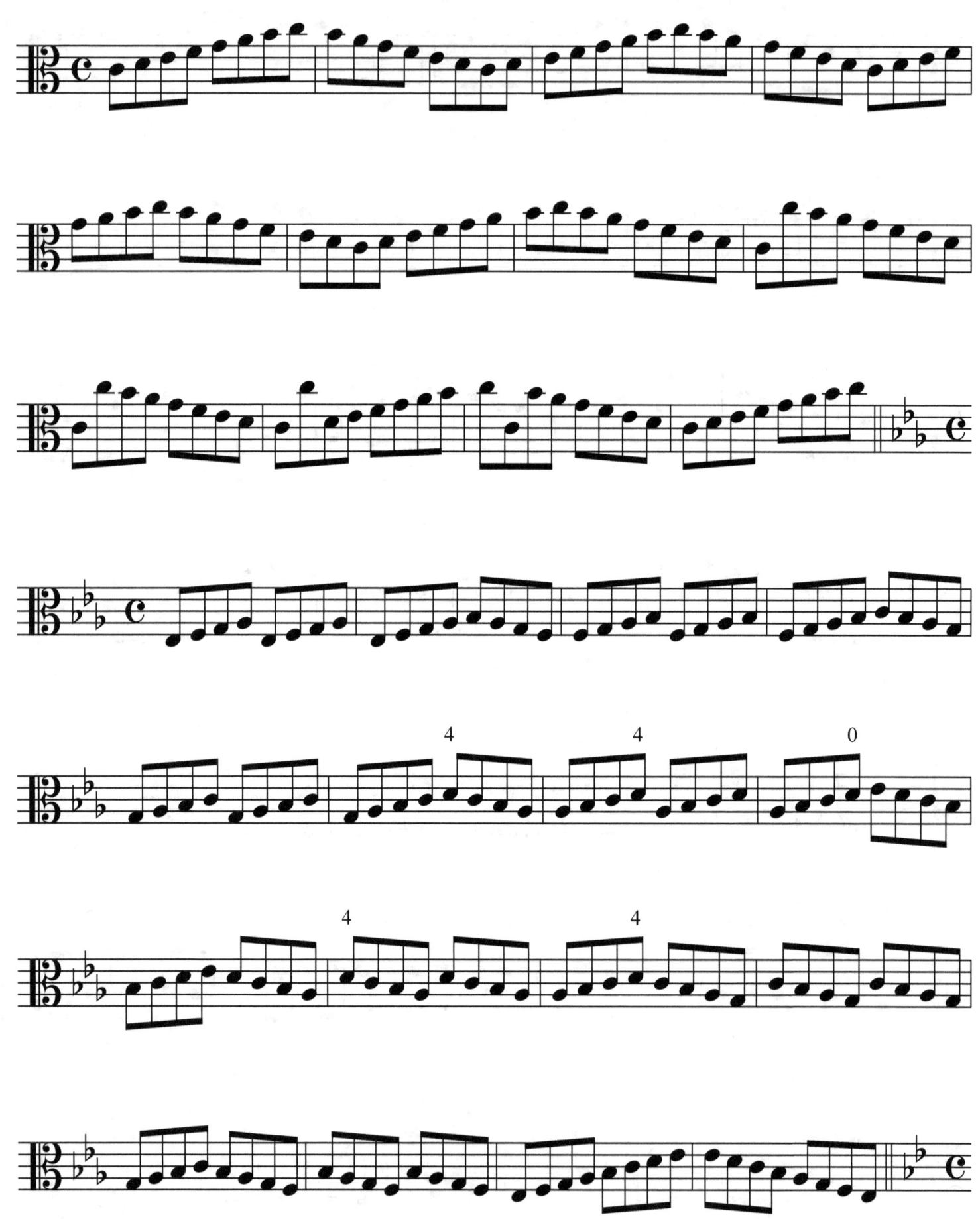

First Position Scale Studies for the Viola, Book One

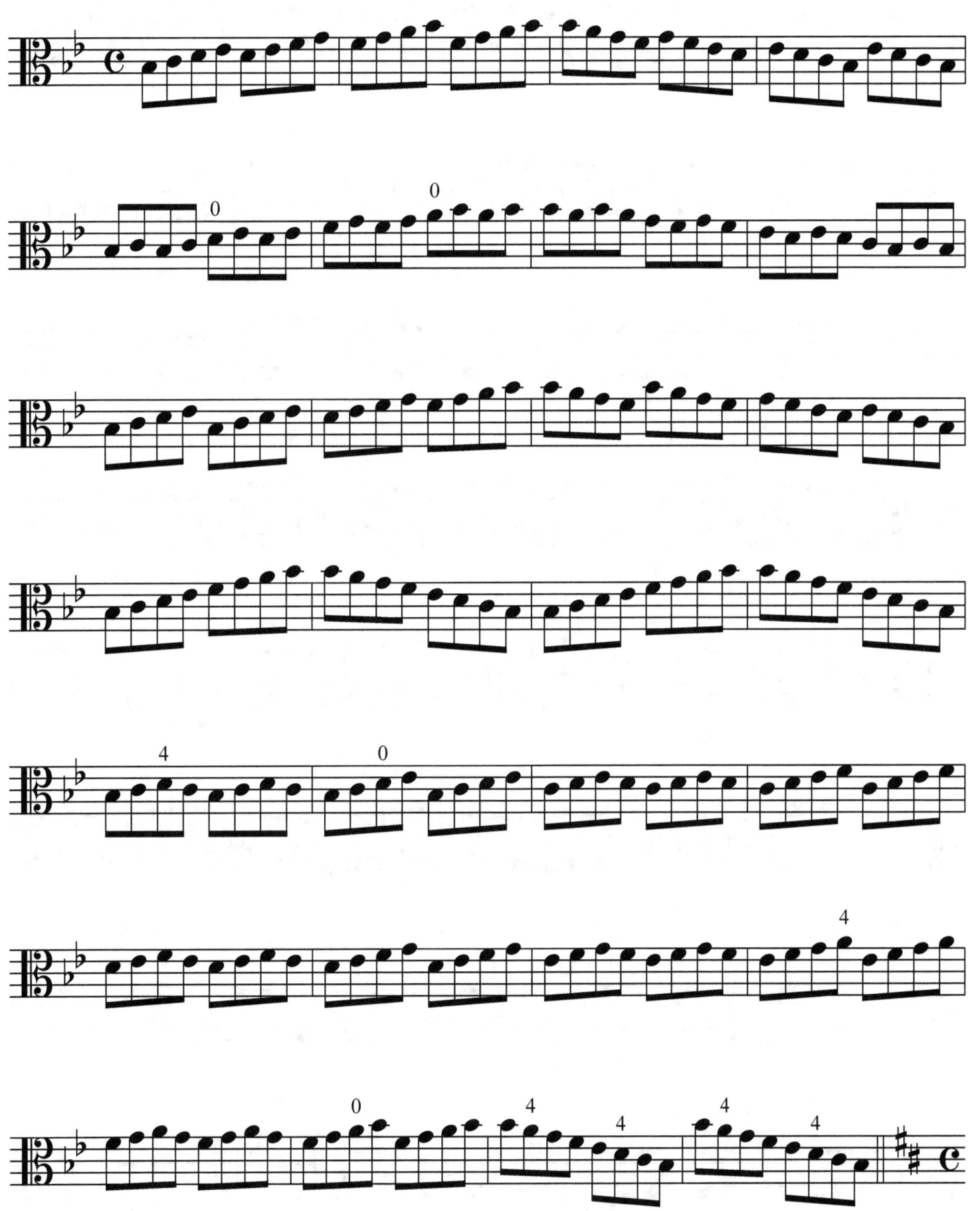

46 First Position Scale Studies for the Viola, Book One

©2017 C. Harvey Publications All Rights Reserved.

First Position Scale Studies for the Viola, Book One

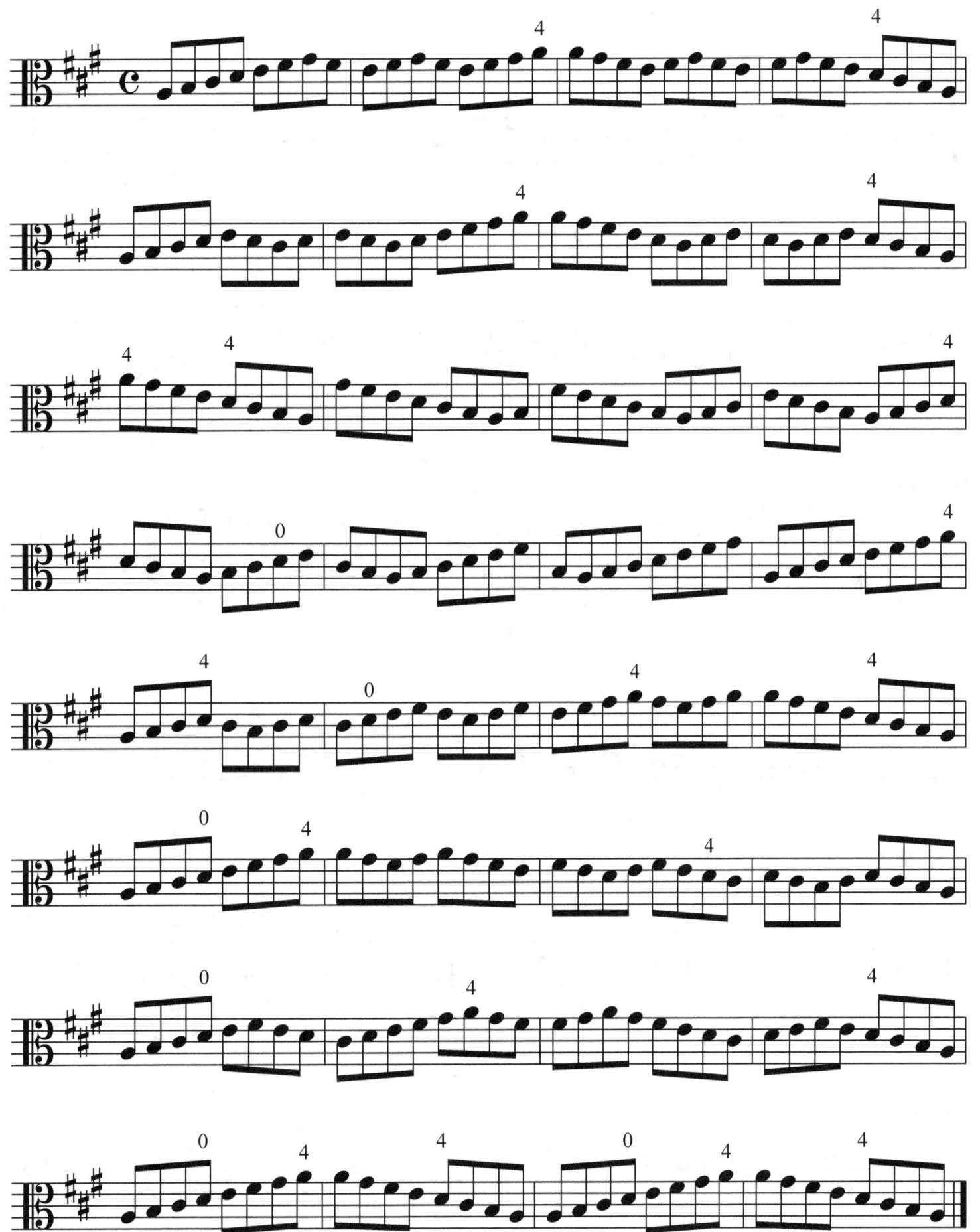

Major Scales in First Position

C Major

D♭ Major

D Major

E♭ Major

E Major

F Major

©2017 C. Harvey Publications All Rights Reserved.

First Position Scale Studies for the Viola, Book One

G♭ Major

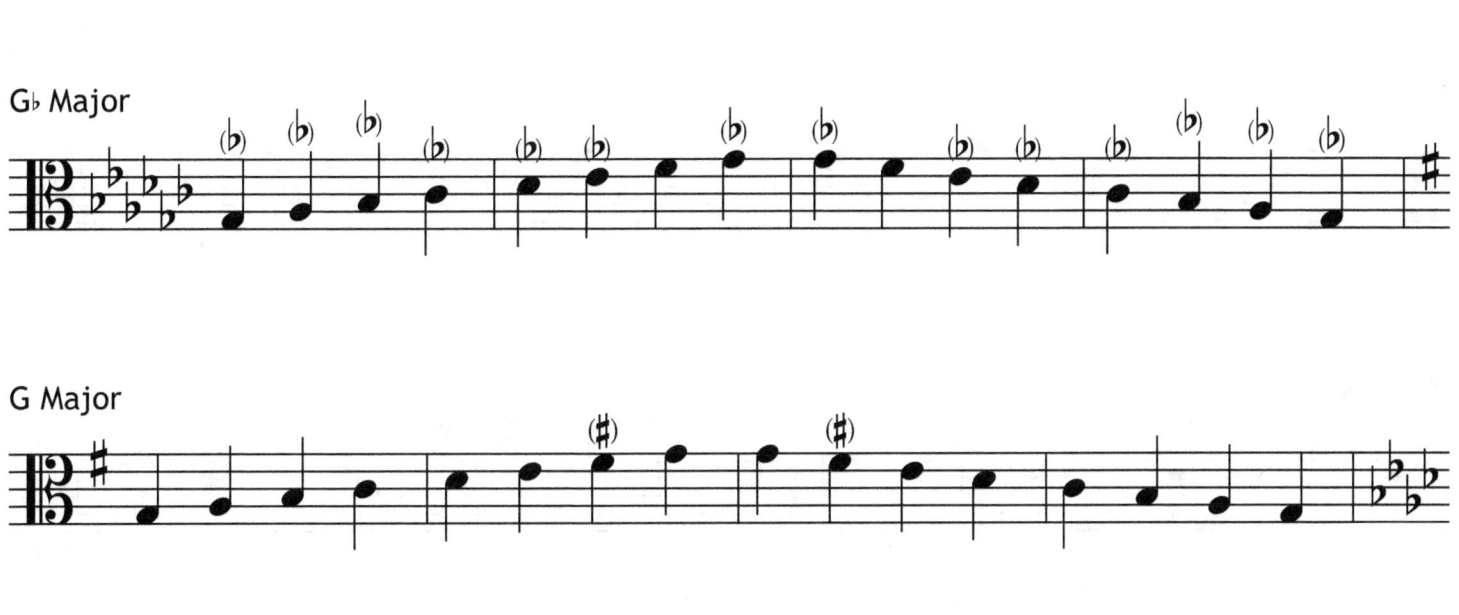

G Major

A♭ Major

A Major

B♭ Major

B Major

©2017 C. Harvey Publications All Rights Reserved.

C Major

D♭ Major

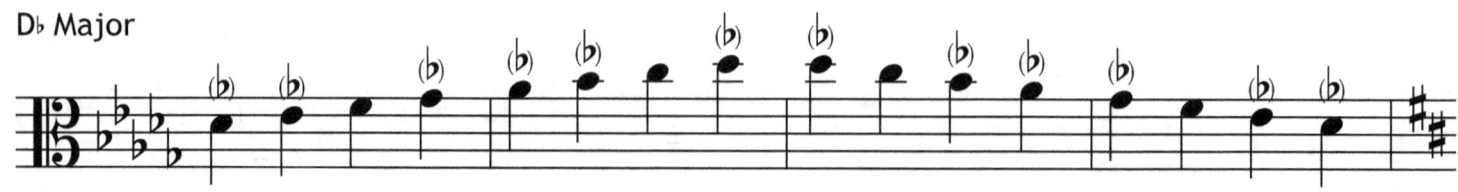

D Major

E♭ Major

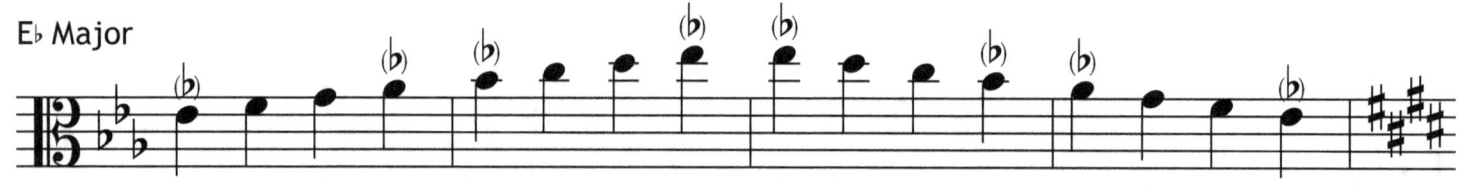

E Major

F Major

Major Arpeggios in First Position